Spots

Written by James Bliss
Illustrations by Amy Wummer

We got red spots on the pot.

We got red spots on the chair.

We got blue spots on the cot.

We got blue spots on the bear.

We got yellow spots on the dots.

We got yellow spots on the stairs.

We got spots everywhere!